REFLECTIONS:

Psychological & Spiritual Images of the Heart

Photographs by George R. Merrill

Text by Robert J. Wicks

PAULIST PRESS
New York and Mahwah, N.J.

Library of Congress Cataloging-in-Publication Data

Merrill, George R., 1934-
Reflections: psychological & spiritual images of the heart/
photographs by George R. Merrill; text by Robert J. Wicks.
p. cm.
ISBN 0-8091-3127-7
1. Spiritual life. 2. Heart—Religious aspects—Christianity
I. Wicks, Robert J. II. Title
BV4501.2.M46 1990
242—dc20 89-39803
CIP

Published by Paulist Press
997 Macarthur Boulevard
Mahwah, NJ 07430

Printed and bound in the
United States of America

PSYCHOLOGICAL & SPIRITUAL IMAGES OF THE HEART

Foreword

Whenever I experience God playing in my heart, I feel excitement and wonder. I am never really clear what has happened except that I begin to see old things in new ways. The whole of the experience seems more than the sum of its parts and the more I ponder the experience, the more I discover in it.

Some meetings, whether of light and object, thought and word, or of persons, seems at first fortuitous. They finally, however, reveal themselves as benevolent conspiracies to awaken us to God's presence in everything that is and that happens.

My sense is that Bob Wicks and I met because God was playing in our hearts. Each of us was feeling an urgency to express a "something," while not clear, certainly compelling. Bob crafted this urgency in words and I in photographic images. As we responded to God's play in our hearts, we wrote and imaged separately and then began to talk together as we became curious about each other's spiritual journey.

By following our separate allurements – to write and to image in this case – a fortuitous meeting revealed a benevolent conspiracy and we became, in a small way, co-creators with God.

Our wish is that these words and images will be a helpful reminder of what is so easily forgotten – that God benevolently conspires to touch us in all things in every way.

George Merrill

A Brief Guide

Artists paint both what their eyes see and what their hearts feel. With words, writers do the same. Yet, both visual portrayals lie dormant until actively encountered by another. And when this happens, new meaning moves from the darkness into the light.

The photographs and words that follow are meant to stimulate thoughts, images, and feelings. They are also designed to encourage reflection on our own behavior in light of the information that is uncovered.

There are no "right" or "wrong" reactions to each statement and the visual image which is its companion. There are only our own *personal* responses.

How we respond can potentially tell us much about our views of self, others and God. All we need to do is find a place apart, quiet down, pray for God's grace, look at one or two of the illustrations and their accompanying statements or questions, and reflect for 15 or 20 minutes.

Such a process may stimulate many personal responses, and so space is provided to those of us who find writing or journaling of help. The four general questions that might be helpful to address in writing down our responses and reactions to the visual stimuli are:

What thoughts came to mind as I looked at the images and the words on each page?

What did I feel as I sat there in quiet and solitude?

What images came to mind during my period of reflection?

Given my thoughts, feelings, and images, how might my behavior be altered in the future?

Once the entire book has been experienced and time (a day, week, month . . . longer) has been allotted for our original thoughts and feelings to recede, additional journeys through our reactions to, and interpretations of, the images and statements may be helpful. While we are looking anew at the material, we can gain further insight this time into the *themes* of our responses—i.e., Do we see the world as threatening, challenging, hopeful? Are there specific people or issues which seem to preoccupy us?

As was previously indicated, writing our reactions—both immediate and delayed—according to the outline and suggested approach above is not necessary. Some of us may find it helpful; some not. The important step, though, is to spend time with God by spending time with ourselves in the reflection and prayer that is stimulated by the material on each page. The importance is that we allow this process to open us to God and the call we are continuously receiving to uncover the presence of the word in our lives . . . the call to be *holy.*

PERSONAL REFLECTIONS

Spiritual awakening dawns when God becomes as real as the problems we face each day.

Being prophetic means, first and foremost, being a *dangerous listener.*

As passive resignation grows into active acceptance, healing begins to take root in our hearts.

Boredom comes from failing to see the community of life within ourselves, and ourselves within God's community.

True prayer often surprises us.

PERSONAL REFLECTIONS

To be truly involved in life is to be prophetic. To be a prophet without experiencing the pain of rejection, failure and misunderstanding is an impossibility.

When we ignore the inner prompting of our hearts to love those whom we don't understand, injustice is frequently one of the sad results.

The amount of real trust we have in God is sometimes best measured by the depth of the doubt and the seriousness of the questions with which we are willing to live.

If laughter is good medicine, then laughing at ourselves and our defenses must surely be healing.

We have only so much energy. What we spend on complaining or defending ourselves cannot be simultaneously available for creativity and joy.

When we truly accept our limits, the opportunity for personal growth and development is almost limitless.

Whereas guilt may push us to do the right thing, love encourages us to do the natural thing.

Spirituality is openness to *relationship* in the deepest, most elegant sense of the term.

The seeds of joy grow best in a field of peace.

Conflicts are natural. In part, they even present us with an opportunity to grow. What we do with the opportunity is up to us.

PERSONAL REFLECTIONS

Failure can often awaken us to life in a much more dramatic way than success ever could.

PERSONAL REFLECTIONS

We must seek the courage to risk being misunderstood until it no longer takes courage.

When our goals threaten instead of inspire us, the result is depression rather than hope and enthusiasm.

PERSONAL REFLECTIONS

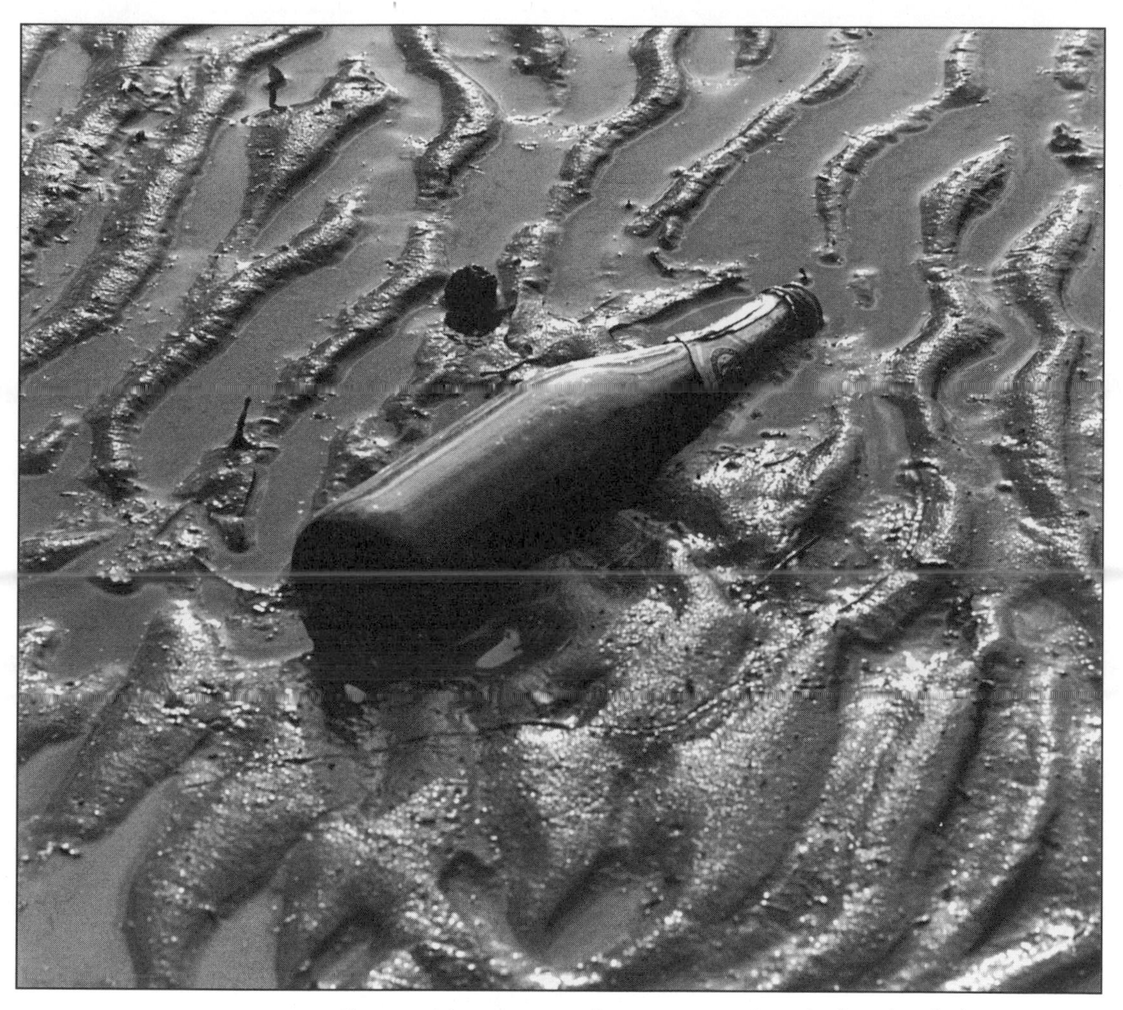

If everything were really everyone else's fault, what little power we would have.

So much energy is spent worrying about the roads we will have to travel tomorrow that there seems to be little concern that the car we bought yesterday is rusting.

It's hard to have vision if we are holding onto the present and still preoccupied with the past.

PERSONAL REFLECTIONS

When we feel hurt by others, our natural inclination is to withdraw. Yet, if we cut ourselves off from others we can become "psychological islands" which are easily swamped by life's inevitable problems.

We are all loyal to at least one negative view of ourselves. What is it?

Losing perspective is easy even when surrounded by interpersonal and material abundance; holiness is knowing this and not being discouraged by it.

Security is like a boat ride with agreeable people. The solace is in having others around us; the problem is we still may be traveling in the wrong direction.

Spiritual challenge is often characterized by the call to hold onto the possible as well as the probable in prayer.

Even though working actively for justice is essential, one of the greatest gifts we can give to a troubled world is the presence of a peaceful heart.

Wrapping ourselves in silence, solitude, and gratitude is a sure way to open our hearts again to perspective and simplicity.

PERSONAL REFLECTIONS

The flame of self-esteem must be first fired from within.

Listening is a lost art that can be gracefully recovered in silence and solitude.

Self-awareness, compassion, and contemplation are different turns on the same road to finding and living the truth.

Depression often occurs when we have forgotten to love the presence of God in all living things . . . including ourselves.

With each discovery of truth about ourselves, we come to a crossroads on our journey toward God. One path leads to denial and despair . . . the other to holiness.

PERSONAL REFLECTIONS

From a psychological perspective, sin is primarily the result of denying, ignoring, or worshiping our own personality.

Spiritual growth occurs only when insight encourages both our hearts and our minds to give up the "advantages" of staying the same for something greater yet unknown.

Humility makes possible the transformation of knowledge into wisdom.

Spiritual intimacy is much more than being close.

All of us have good memories that don't necessarily serve us well in the present.

PERSONAL REFLECTIONS

Patience and a willingness to accept our limitedness allows us to live in peace with the following reality: the emotional bridges we build to others sometimes fall down each time we leave, and have to be rebuilt each time we return.

One of the greatest human paradoxes is that we seem to complain the most about a lack of spiritual passion in our lives at the very same time when we are willing to gamble the least.

Please Note

Another way of employing *Reflections* as a spiritual/journaling guide is in conjunction with either/both of the following Paulist Press books by Robert Wicks:

Availability: The Problem and the Gift
Living Simply in an Anxious World: An Invitation to Perspective

REV. GEORGE R. MERRILL

The Rev. George R. Merrill is a native of Staten Island, NY. An Episcopal priest, he attended Hobart College, the Berkeley Divinity School at Yale and the American Foundation of Religion and Psychiatry in New York City.

He is a Diplomate of the American Association of Pastoral Counselors and a Supervisor of the Association for Clinical Pastoral Education.

He served parishes in New York City and West Hartford, CT, and was the Chief of Chaplaincy Services for the Alcohol and Drug Dependence Division of the Connecticut State Department of Mental Health.

Rev. Merrill is at present on the faculty of the Pastoral Counseling Department, Loyola College in Maryland; the Director of the Baltimore Pastoral Counseling Service; and the Associate Director of the Commission on Pastoral Care and Counseling of the Baltimore Annual Conference of the United Methodist Church.

Rev. Merrill's photography has been exhibited in Annapolis and Baltimore.

He and his wife Jo are avid sailors of the Chesapeake Bay and live in Timonium, Maryland.

DR. ROBERT J. WICKS

Dr. Robert Wicks is Professor and Director of Program Development for Pastoral Counseling at Loyola College in Maryland and on the part-time faculty of Washington Theological Union. He is a graduate of Hahnemann Medical College as well as Fairfield and St. John's Universities. Prior to taking the position at Loyola, he was Director of the Graduate Program in Pastoral Counseling at Neumann College and was on the faculty of Bryn Mawr College's Graduate School of Social Work and Social Research. He also taught in universities and in professional schools of psychology, theology, medicine, and nursing. In addition, he has directed mental health treatment programs in the United States and the Orient.

Dr. Wicks has published numerous books and articles. He is the senior co-editor of the *Clinical Handbook of Pastoral Counseling,* which involves thirty-two Protestant and Catholic scholars from major universities and seminaries across the United States. He is also the author of the widely read book *Availability: The Problem and the Gift.*

Dr. Wicks maintains a private practice in Maryland, is Book Review Editor for the National Association of Catholic Chaplains, is General Editor of Paulist Press' *Integration Books: Studies in Pastoral Psychology, Theology, and Spirituality,* and is a member of the Editorial Board of *Human Development.* His major areas of expertise include the integration of psychology and spirituality and pastoral counseling.